SUPER CUTE!

Baby COWS

by Kari Schuetz

BELLWETHER MEDIA • MINNEAPOLIS, MN

Note to Librarians, Teachers, and Parents:

Blastoff! Readers are carefully developed by literacy experts and combine standards-based content with developmentally appropriate text.

Level 1 provides the most support through repetition of high-frequency words, light text, predictable sentence patterns, and strong visual support.

Level 2 offers early readers a bit more challenge through varied simple sentences, increased text load, and less repetition of high-frequency words.

Level 3 advances early-fluent readers toward fluency through increased text and concept load, less reliance on visuals, longer sentences, and more literary language.

Level 4 builds reading stamina by providing more text per page, increased use of punctuation, greater variation in sentence patterns, and increasingly challenging vocabulary.

Level 5 encourages children to move from "learning to read" to "reading to learn" by providing even more text, varied writing styles, and less familiar topics.

Whichever book is right for your reader, Blastoff! Readers are the perfect books to build confidence and encourage a love of reading that will last a lifetime!

This edition first published in 2014 by Bellwether Media, Inc.

No part of this publication may be reproduced in whole or in part without written permission of the publisher. For information regarding permission, write to Bellwether Media, Inc., Attention: Permissions Department, 5357 Penn Avenue South, Minneapolis, MN 55419.

Library of Congress Cataloging-in-Publication Data

Schuetz, Kari.
 Baby cows / by Kari Schuetz.
  p. cm. – (Blastoff! readers. Super cute!)
 Audience: K to grade 3.
 Summary: "Developed by literacy experts for students in kindergarten through grade three, this book introduces baby cows to young readers through leveled text and related photos"– Provided by publisher.
 Includes bibliographical references and index.
 ISBN 978-1-60014-924-5 (hardcover : alk. paper)
 1. Calves–Juvenile literature. 2. Cattle–Juvenile literature. 3. Animals–Infancy–Juvenile literature. I. Title.
 SF205.S38 2014
 636.207–dc23
                                                              2013009636

Table of Contents

Calves!

Baby cows are called calves. They live on farms.

Heifer calves
are females.
Bull calves
are males.

Time With Mom

A female cow has her first calf at age 2. She has one calf every year after that.

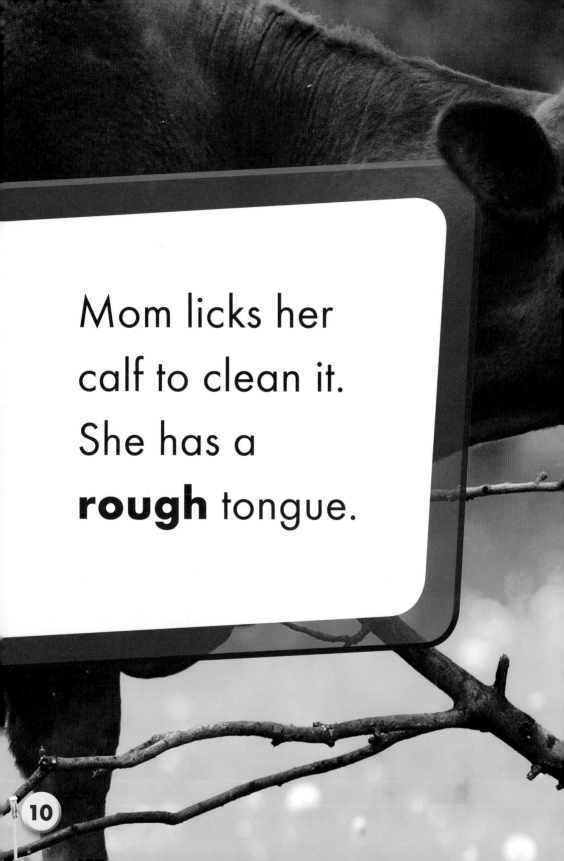

Mom licks her calf to clean it. She has a **rough** tongue.

Mom makes
milk for her
calf to drink.

On the Farm

Sometimes a farmer feeds a calf from a bottle.

An older calf eats hay or grains by a barn.

It also **grazes** on grasses in the **pasture**. Then it chews its **cud**.

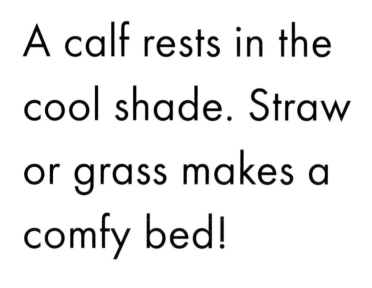

A calf rests in the cool shade. Straw or grass makes a comfy bed!

Glossary

cud–food that is chewed again after being in the belly

grazes–feeds on grasses and other plants

pasture–a field with grasses for grazing

rough–not smooth

To Learn More

AT THE LIBRARY

Alexander, Heather. *All Around the Farm.* New York, N.Y.: Parachute Press/DK Pub., 2007.

Editors of Kingfisher. *Baby Animals On the Farm.* New York, N.Y.: Kingfisher, 2010.

Sexton, Colleen. *The Life Cycle of a Cow.* Minneapolis, Minn.: Bellwether Media, 2011.

ON THE WEB

Learning more about cows is as easy as 1, 2, 3.

1. Go to www.factsurfer.com.

2. Enter "cows" into the search box.

3. Click the "Surf" button and you will see a list of related Web sites.

With factsurfer.com, finding more information is just a click away.

Index

The images in this book are reproduced through the courtesy of: Nate Allred, front cover, pp. 4-5, 14-15; Biosphoto/ SuperStock, pp. 6-7; Lynn M. Stone/ Kimball Stock, pp. 8-9; Juniors/ SuperStock, pp. 10-11; Dave Hughes, pp. 12-13; Rachel Dunn, pp. 16-17; Ivan Kmit, pp. 18-19; Emholk, pp. 20-21.

DATE DUE

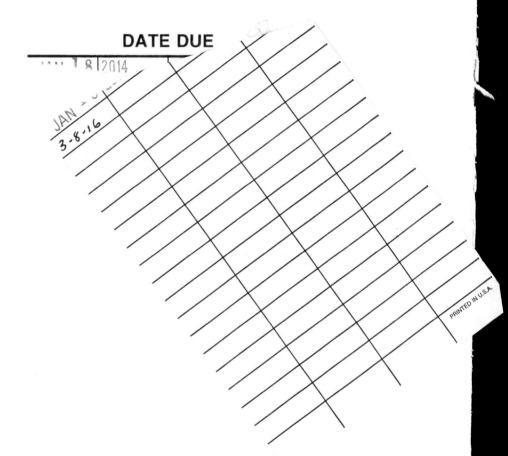

JAN
8 2014

3-8-16

PRINTED IN U.S.A.